Words in Progress

JB Fray

Presentation by *BookLeaf Publishing*

Web: www.bookleafpub.com

E-mail: info@bookleafpub.com

ISBN: 9789358312447

First edition 2023

I dedicate this to my Soleil, who keeps me warm when I'm alone and lost. To Solange, my mother.

ACKNOWLEDGEMENT

I thank God for the gift of writing and for the gift of wisdom. I thank my mother for all the things that are fabulous, beautiful, wonderful, classy and driven in me. She makes me always want more. She makes me always want to be gracious, stylish and wonderfully driven. I thank my husband who believes me to be wise even when I am a full-on mess and contradiction to how he sees me. I thank my husband for always breathing his life and light into me and as Mother Earth, I turn it into something wonderful for us to live in. I thank my daughter for being my constant inspiration to do better, to go longer, to go faster and to get it done.

PREFACE

This collection of poems is about looking at the past through the eyes of my ancestors right up to my mother's last words to me, "I can not do anything for you Jenny, my brain is leaving." To me, it all starts with God, My mother, me and then my lovely daughter. It is important for me to be my mother's daughter now more than ever as she only wants me to live the best life I could ever have. I take what goodness God gave to my mother in her blood and run as fast as I can with it. I pass it on to my daughter and hope that she takes it with grace until the day I can no longer do anything for her and her babies. This collection of poems is my healing and my freedom to live, lead and experience the life of my dreams.

Dear You

Dear You
It can sometimes feel like,
I was born to be psyched up
to be left behind.
Sometimes it feels like,
I was born to dream
Big for myself
But only get
The second kind
Or even sometimes
Worst
The 3rd and fourth kind.
I ask for what
I want
And I get something else.
I get a twisted

3rd of what I want.
I get some of what
I desire.
Like a similar picture
But not at all.
I pray to you,
I cry to you,
I beg you.
Truthfully.......
Sometimes, I get something
But not the thing.
Then....
I look up,
And you have heard
Someone else's prayer,
You've answered
Someone else's desires
You've answered.
I often wonder
Do you hear?
Do you love me?
Do you like me?
Do you see me?
Can you bless me too?
I know you love, I know you care,
I know you are there.
I've seen you and heard
In others' lives.
I've seen you in full

Color.
I've seen you save people
And call them back.
I've watched you
Be on time.
I've seen you work
Your touch for people
Who blatantly disobey
Your decrees.
I've seen you
Give
Favor to the unfavorable.
Grace to the rude
Abundance to the thief.
Majesty to the mean.
Freedom to the oppressor.
And
Opulence to the indignant.
But-

Still asking can you hear me

Me-
Who tries and works
To live by your word.
Do you know
I'm here?
Do you hear,
My prayer?
My prayer of Why not me?
How come not me?
I'm not sure anymore,
If I should even have desires.
I'm not sure anymore,
If I should even dream.
I'm tired of wanting, desiring and dreaming.
It's exhausting.
I'm making half of what I want.
I'm living pieces of what I want.
I'm feeling unloved, unnoticed, unheard.

I want to wake and know You did it all. You are
doing it all for me, as I see you do for others.
Bless me with your swift love and attention.
Bless me with quick entrances to happiness,
health, wealth, peace prosperity, abundance,
opulence and ease.
Not just for me from You, but for my family and
my family's family. For now until the end of
time.
Breathe all the goodness into me and pass it
down to my people's people.
I know You can hear me.

I believe you can hear me.

I know you can do it and you are doing it all,
right now!
I can feel it.
I can feel and believe the change. I can sense
your work and I can see the universe facing me
and blessing me and my posterity at this point.
Thank You,
Thank You,
Thank You.

Although....
I'm still asking are you there, can you hear me?
Can you see me?

The feelings of change and other weirdness

It's changing.
I believe you are doing exceedingly and
abundantly above all that I've prayed for. I can
feel the freedom and joy.
I can smell the fresh clean air.
I can feel the mist of the beach and the warmth
of the past Sun.
I can taste the savory and sweet love of You.
I can hear the music play as I walk up to accept
another award for my contribution to life.
I can see you, in everything that is warm and
beautiful in my life. In my babies, in my
husband, in my work, in my new beautiful
house.
I honor You in bended knee and because of this,
You love me and bless me and protect me and
my posterity.
I am grateful
that
I am surrounded by your
Favor.
That is all I ever wanted.
But instead I get….
Jealousy.

Jealousy is what I got,
Is what I'm dealing with.
Dealing with the Jealousy.

I mean of jealousy in me.

Of a life I wish was meant for me.
A life I desire to be.
A life I inquire with you about.
A Life that somehow, I go without.
A life now turned inward to Jealousy and
questions like, "Why not me Lord?"
"Why am I not special enough, why don't you
choose me?"
I have the call in me, I hear the call in me. I
know what I'm meant to be,
but it does not come with ease,
support or any true sense of freedom.
It just comes with
Jealousy in me.
Fear in me.
Doubt in me.
Hiding in me.
Shame in me.
It comes with
Missing the sun.
It comes with
Him, her and me.
And we-

Are all doing the same thing.
Moving in the same lane.
We are all stomping on one another.

I don't even get started on my venture and
another is right on me
in the same wave,
and winning,
while I'm still spinning.
Spinning in the wave.

Where are you?
Are you here with me too?
I'm looking for signs of you.

Nope…
I'm just confused.
Not hopeless, just abused.
Not faithless, just confused.
These feelings of change are confusing and
painful.
Please help me, help him, help her, help
them......

Are you there?

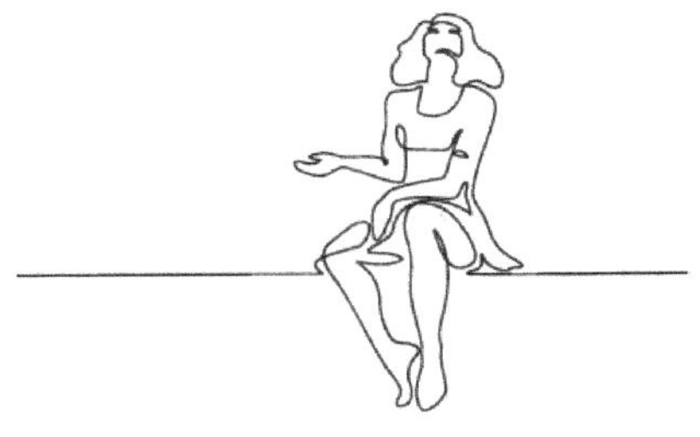

Where are you?
I'm looking, I'm feeling
and I'm believing.
But all I get is broken,
half dreams or maybe some token
Of what I mean.
But not close enough to my
True dream.
Where are you?
Cause the jealousy is starting to settle in.
But, I know better
Jealousy won't ever get me nowhere near to
clearer weather,
Sunny warm weather.

Where are you?
I'm looking, I'm feeling
and I'm believing.
But all I get is broken,
half dreams or maybe some token
Of what I mean.
But not close enough to my
True dream.
Where are you?
Cause the jealousy is starting to settle in.
But, I know better
Jealousy won't ever get me nowhere near to
clearer weather,
Sunny warm weather.

So now I'm just unsure, unclear and impure of
who I am and what I feel.
I Am not clear.
I Am not sure.
I am not sure what to be anymore.
I am not sure what women are anymore.
Is she strong,
Is she beautiful,
Is she warm?
Is she still a mom, wife, lover, friend, daughter,
sister and more?
Wait…..
I know this.

I know that I want to live my dreams in full
Color.
Outside and in front of me.
Right here where it should all be.
Every good and pure dream that is me,
Every good and pure passion is good for me.
Every desire that I longed to be.
I long to be.
Long to be?
To be?
To be who and why?
Be me.
What is me?
Me?
That person who can see
And hear with clarity,
Who they ought to be.
But, is that easy?
Is that where you be?
Can you hear me?
Can you hear me, ask for success, happiness,
health, wealth, peace and prosperity for me and
My posterity?
Can you hear me?
Can you see me, watching others get what I've
been praying to be?
Praying to be?
Yes, me. Praying, longing for you to hear me
and then come in me.

Praying to be worthy.
To be someone who you choose to be glory.
Being someone who is full of your glory and
your story.
I long to be fulfilled and embodied by
Your lovely majesty.
Your majesty that…
Opens lanes, trains and planes.
Planes full of plans that you tamed.
Tamed just for me to be, do and have.
Have you forgotten your promise to me?
You promised I would know the truth and be set
with
You.
It would be nice.
So nice.
It would be nice if…
It would be nice if it could all change overnight.
If the life that I pray about for me and my
family, just showed up. If my daughter's dreams
would just come to her with ease. Come to her
and through her with your ease. If she could
experience goodness, I know that she is meant to
be.
It would be nice if my husband's true dreams and
desires would just come to him overnight in the
blink of an eye. With the blink of your eye.
It would be nice if I did not feel like…
Like…

Like, I'm the one who ruins it for everyone. That
I'm the secret wrong in the rum.
I'm the secret badness that is holding it all
undone.
It would be nice to also live, lead and breathe the
life of my dreams.
Dreams that you gave me.
It would be nice to know you love me.
Are you there?

Your child too

Love me like you love the others that are cold
and callous to me.
Love me, see me, open roads for me.
Protect me,
let them know that I belong to you.
Let them know that they all should give her the
best of everything.
Give her the best of me, because she is one of
the best of me.
It would be nice to be free,
It would be nice to be successful at what I
choose to be,
It would be nice to be all the parts of me and still
be.
It would be nice to live a life of ease, opulence
mixed completely with you hearing me and
guiding me directly.
It would be nice to dream Big and get even
bigger results.
It would be nice to live in your light.
It would be nice....
It would be nice to live freely.
It would be nice to take a step forward and know
you are there to guide me and lead me and
protect me. Even make a way for me. It would

be nice to have forces gathered to help me and
my family.
It would be nice to have momentum moving in
the right direction.
It would be nice to clearly hear you, see you,
touch you and embody you.
Where are you?
Love me,
Your Child

Dear My Child

Didn't you see me in the song you wrote?
Didn't you hear me in the lesson you taught?
Didn't you feel me in his touch on your face?
Didn't you taste me in the Kremas you made?
Didn't you smell me in the air of Spring and
Summer?
Didn't you hear me in the voice of K.Dot?
Didn't you feel me on your skin that the sun
kissed?
Didn't you feel the warmth of the sun through
the window in the passenger seat of the white
truck?
I was there.
I told you to make that right, Didn't you hear?
I asked you to stay when Steph, "Are you sure
you want to leave?"
You left anyway.
I whispered to you that night in the Range
Rover.
I whispered to you that night at Mercy Hospital.

I whispered, are you listening?
I'm always with you, are you paying attention?

I held you and hugged you, when you wept
cause you thought he was the one who would
change your life.
He did change your life,

I was there jumping with joy, when he surprised
your life
And said, "I want to show you that miracles and
dreams do come true."
I was there when she came, a blessing from me.
I gave you the best celebratory union.
I pushed you on to freedom.
I gave you the strength you didn't know you had.
I blessed you and your family with love and
protection when they attacked physically and
spiritually.
I covered you and them when the world changed
again.
I gave you the words and prayers and the spirit
of prayer to keep going.
I gave him more, which gave you more.
I gave you steel in your back and quiet in your
mind and peace in your heart when the Queen
said,
"I am no longer a use to you."
I'm giving you words and visions.
I'm giving you the keys to the next 50.
I'm blessing you and him and them with more.
Be obedient, talk to me, trust me, do my work.

I will live in thee.
I am living in thee.
Don't be afraid.
Wear me in thee, Wear me on thee.
And allow me to breathe through you.

I'm back asking, Dear You.

What am I doing wrong?
Have I offended you?
Please tell me, I won't do it again.
Please tell me how to better please you and serve
you.
Sometimes…
Sometimes, I feel like I'm bad luck.
Sometimes I feel like I'm not enough.
Sometimes I feel like I'm not worthy.
I have dreams and desires and goals.
I'm living them in pieces and fractions, never a
whole pie.
For fear of you, I don't do too much, because I
don't want you to
Leave.
But, even when I know I'm following you and
being in reverence for you, your name, your son
I'm still just getting by.
I'm grateful to you for many things, but still I
strain.
Please send us help.
Please send us miracles and grace.
Please send us victory.
Please send us innovative direction that is loud
and clear.

Please send us our dreams, desires and goals
with ease this time.
Please release us from the bandage of obscurity,
lack of will, insecurity and bondage, bandage.
Free us, bless us, accept us.
Lead us to the spaces I know you are in.
Lead us to Trinity.
Lead us to Victory.
I'm back asking for your direction.

Solèy la Leve

The sun once told me, "Your name is all you
have." While it shined so brightly on me.
I think I was ten.
She told me to shine bright through your smile.
She told me to shine bright through your grit.
She told me to shine bright through your
heartache.
She told me to shine bright through my work
and through my hospitality and through my
sisterhood and through my daughterhood and
through my walk and my talk and my name.
I would look up to her light shining brightly with
one hand,
Trying to shield me from her undeniable warm
rays.
Solèy la limen lavi mwen.
The Sun lit up my life and gave me direction,
even when it was in opposite directions.
The Sun would dress me up.
The Sun would dress herself up.
The Sun would be it all.
I welcomed the Sun.
I look for the Sun.
I am living in the Sun and remembering all the
warmth and lessons.

I am remembering, my hands are made of the
sun, my style and grace are of the sun. My
entrance into a room brings the Sun with me.
I will always remember my name, and I will
always bring the Sun with me.
Solèy la gives me energy.
I am forty and
Solèy la leve.

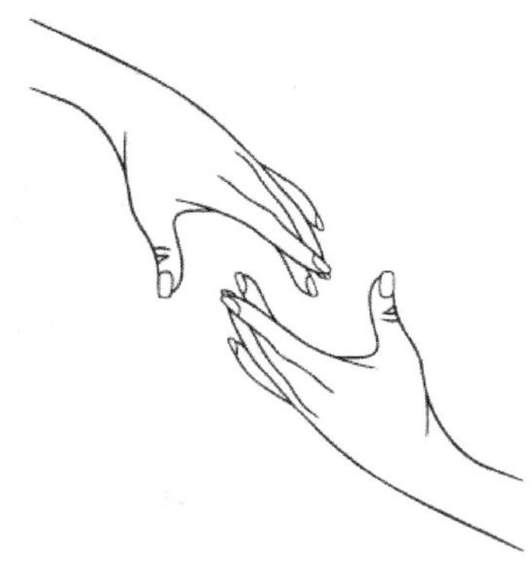

Nouvou Jou

Here is my prayer and request.
Take the weakness from me.
Take the fear from me.
Take the doubt from me.
Take the insecurity from me.
Take the worry from me.
Take the feeling of rejection.
Take away the procrastination in me.
Take away the laziness in me.
Take anything away in me,
That stands in the way of me being the best.
Take away anything in me
That stands in the way of me being as bright as
the sun.
Give me vigor and resolve.
Give me bravery and confidence.
Give me security and stability.
Give me peace and assurance.
Give me acceptance and encouragement.
Give me the ambition to win.
Give me diligence and industrious ideas.
Give me objectives and purpose with a vision.
Give me all that I need to win.
All that I need to win wherever I go and
wherever I am.

It's a new day and I am ready.
I am ready to be filled with new emotions about
me and my life.
Let's go! Let's get it!

Life Dysmorphia

I learned that,
dysmorphia means:
a mental health condition where a person can
spend a lot of time worrying about flaws in their
appearance.

That made me think. That made me ask myself,
"Do I have Life Dysmorphia?"
"Am I worrying about the appearance of flaws
in my life?"
"Am I worrying about the appearance of flaws
in the things that I do?"
"Am I dysmorphing my life?"
Maybe I am.
Maybe I spend too much time thinking about
what is not there
as opposed to
thinking about the beauty that is actually
showing up in my life daily.
I think it's time to change that sad depiction of
my waking life.
I think it's time to see the good in my life as a
blessing.
I think it's time to believe and know that my life
is wonderful.

I think it's time to have faith that I am right
where I am supposed to be,
doing what I am supposed to be doing
and
that all things are working out for me.
I know that this will be hard because it looks
like everyone is…
Everyone is living it up and having a good time:
In their big cars,
In their big house,
With their great careers, that gives them great
freedom.
It seems like their lives are made of the stuff that
my dreams are made of.
But, wait?
Is that life dysmorphia?
Maybe I AM living the life of my dreams too?
Maybe I am not looking at what is good?
Or maybe I should at least try and look at what
is good?

What's good?
I've got air in my lungs.
Dreams in my head.
A husband that loves and likes me.
A daughter growing as beautiful as a Japanese
Cherry Tree.
Writing that comes to me straight from above.
Food that I love to cook and eat.

Family to laugh with.
Friends that make me laugh out loud.
Students that respect my space.
A girl's empowerment group that is fun and growing.
New ideas to lead my life with.
A horizon that gives me visions and goals.
Another day to get it all right.
I don't want to see my life in blurs and false narratives.
I want to see my life in the pure platinum that I was given.
I want to see, live, taste, smell my life in clarity.

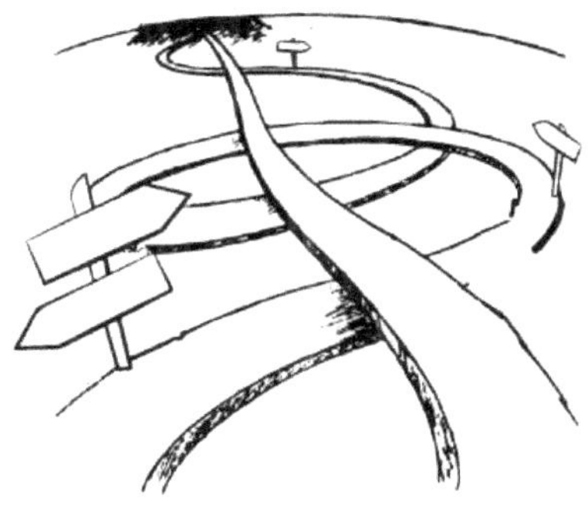

What I am not vs. What I AM

I AM not a hustler.
I do not move like a thief.
I plan and pray.
I work and pray.
I am not that bitch.
I am not a bitch or a hoe.
I AM a creator and maker.
I take seeds
plant seeds and bring forth fruits,
Vegetables, beautiful cherry trees,
And aromatic lavender fields.
I am not naked.
I am not in need of
All eyes on my secrets.

I AM selective about what I share and show.
I AM in need of a protective, providing, guiding,
loving and warm husband.

I AM me.
I AM out here, trying to be the best me that I can
be.
I AM out here,
Praying,
Believing,

Working,
Striving and Thriving,
Creating and so much more.

I AM more than what the world tries to tell me
that I am.

I AM all that I can and want to be.

I AM whatever I say I AM.
I AM THAT I AM me.

Jealousy

I'm jealous.
I don't want to be,
but I am.
I am jealous.
I am jealous of the ease,
that seems to follow you around.
I am jealous of what seems to be
success that happens for you
and not for me.
I'm jealous of what you get to do and be.
I'm jealous that I wanted that life too,
But stuck with being number two.

I am jealous and I don't want to be,
but I am.

I am jealous of how fast you move.
I am jealous of how smart you are,
you always seem to know what to do.
I am jealous of the mistakes that you escape.
I am jealous of the rules you break.
I am jealous that you can still move and shake.
While I'm stuck with just the shake.

Imposter syndrome.

That is what is happening.
Happened to make me jealous.
Imposters live in the dark in corners
and lie to themselves about who
Are.
Syndromes, symptoms and conditions.
I created them all.
I created them to characterize my life
In comparisons,
in comparison to who
I am standing next to you.

I don't want to be jealous.
I want to be me
I fully decree,
that
I'm creating new conditions.
I'm creating new manifestations.
I'm creating new directions.
I'm creating new indications.
I am moving into assuredly me.
I am moving into an incredible me.
I am moving into a distinguished me.
I am moving into a smart me.
I am moving into a wiser me.
I am moving into a truthful me.
I am moving into a winning me.

I am not jealous,
I AM working on being….
Authentic..
Powerful..
Clear..
True..
Fair
and
Kind to me.
Because, who am I fooling?
I can only be me
and
that is how it is going to be.

Hello My Love,

Hello My love,
They say timing is everything.
They say motivation plus inspiration
And focus get you all your dreams.
They say it's important
To have a vision, my love.
Are you listening, my love?
They say it's important to
Recognize that you are
A beautiful wonderful being,
A beautiful smart and wise
Wonderful King.

Hello My Love,
I'm in love with a God.
Who is never at odds,
With what can be like a trap.
So he makes choices that makes
Him get back.
Back to the winning,
Back to the planning and winning.
Back to the victory
With full respect and command.
Never a failure,
Only a winner.

Hello My Love,
I fell in love
With a man
Who was sent from above,
Sent from our past.
He was king
And
He leads me to all of our dreams
Cause he got wings.
He gives us precision, protection
And provides us with none of the lies.
He's got perception of depth,
He's patient and kind
With all of our lives.

Hello My Love,
I see you with all of my heart.
I hear you with all of my fingers.
I feel you with all of my might.
I taste you with all of my passion.
I smell you with all of my love.

Hello My Love,
I am your patience,
I am your prudence,
I am your devotion,
I am your spot.

Hello My Love,

I know you work hard
And
You've been scarred.
But that don't mean jack
Cause
I got your back.

Hello My Love,
Your green eyes
Send me abound
And
I'll always be down
To go this way
Or
That.
Cause, we go way back.

Hello My Love,
The time is now.
For you to get down
Down in the work.
To get all your worth.
Just make it work.
Get you a vision
With a true intention,
To give a mission.

Hello My Love,
It's me your Queen

And
In love, we will be
Through eternity.

With Much Love and Respect
Your Queen at Best!

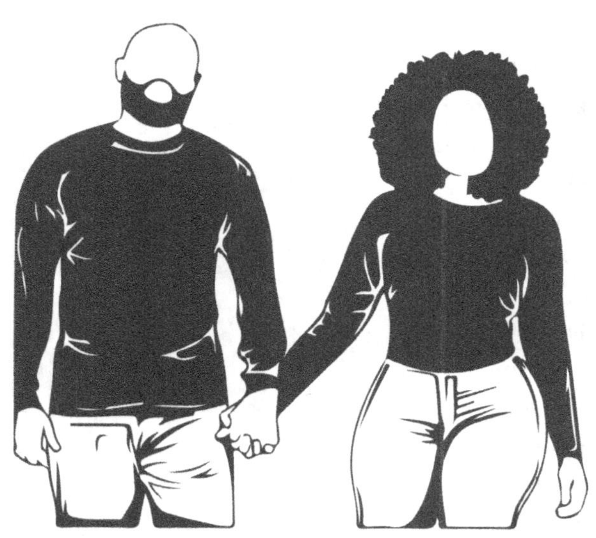

Questions, Lies and Truths

You want to be like me.
I want to be like you.

Are we confused?
Are we afraid?
Are we lying to one another?
Are we destroying one another?

What are we confused about?
What are we afraid of?
What happens if I can be you?
What happens when you can be me?
What then?

Will we truly understand?
Will we truly understand one another?
Will we be kind to one another?
Will we find the human in one another?
Will I give you a chance my brother?
Will I forgive you my sister?

When will the arguing stop?
When will the anxiety stop?
When will the beatings stop?
When will the coercion stop?

When will the conversions stop?
When will the waring stop?
When will the denial of rights stop?

Where will we meet?
Where will we drop our bags and shake hands?
Where?
Where will the peace begin?
Where will it all end?
Where do we begin?
Where will we make amends?
Where will the roads lead to understanding and
respect?

Who will decide?
Who will take a chance and forgive first?
Who will say, this is too much pain, war and loss
of life?
Who will let it all go for the good of all?
Who will remember when, remember when we
laughed together and prayed differently
together?
Who will be the first to put their pride aside to
lead the way to peace?
Who will say, "Enough is enough this is all
fucked up. This is just too much."
Who will decide that our kids are more
important than just pride?

How much will it take?
How much will it cost?
How much do we give?
How can we go on?
Go on hating one another, disposing of each
other, lying to one another, stealing from each
other, lying about each other or just plain being
afraid of one another.
How can we accept the garbage?
How can we accept the separation of human
emotion and life?

Why won't we stop? -
Stop being ego-driven.
Why won't we allow ourselves to be just as we
are?
Why won't we respect one another?
Why won't we face the truth?

The truth is we just don't like ourselves.
The truth is that we want to dominate.
The truth is we are scared of them, so we make
others hate them as well.
The truth is we have no respect for ourselves, so
we easily don't respect our neighbor.
The truth is we can change.
Change on a dime.
The truth is we are all hurting from something.
The truth is there is laughter and joy out there.

The truth is life is good, no matter what!
The truth is we can change and love and like one another.
The truth is always better than the lies we spin.

Marlene, Lynn and Kelly

Life is funny, you don't know when things will
suddenly change.
One day, you are in your 3D apartment talking
to your best friend in 3C through the window.
The next day, you're sitting on the steps of 93
Florence Avenue laughing with your friend and
her sisters.
The last day, you and your cousin are staying up
late at night giggling and laughing on the floor
of your bedroom with the blue carpet.
Those worlds would collide sometimes and
other times they would come together like a
velvety cake.
They all made me feel special and loved.
They all made me feel like,
I was their best friend no matter how far we
were apart.
Two were friends and one was a cousin.
I miss them all.
I miss their differences in what made them
special.
I miss how they all blessed my life.
I wish that we still hung out.
I wish that we still knew one another so well,
That our children knew one another.

I wish that life didn't change so fast.
I wish that I could apologize if I ever made them
feel weird.
I wish that we were still close friends.

I wish that you all knew that I miss our talks and
our giggles.
If you ever read this,
I pray that your lives are filled with
Peace, love, light and many blessings.

The boys who listened

You know who you are.
You know we stayed on the phone till 3 in the
morning.
You know that we had our own stories.
You know that we shared our cultures.

You know who you are.
You made me forget that I was not the prettiest.
You made me forget that I was lonely.
You made me forget that I was lost.
You made me forget that I was not the smartest.
You made me forget that sometimes life gets
hard.

You know who you are.
You made me remember that I was beautiful.
You made me remember that I can do anything.
You made me remember that I was never alone.
You made me remember that I was more than
just a pretty face.
You made me remember that sometimes life is
amazing and kind.

You know who you are.
You let me drive your car.

You picked me up from work at the mall.
You made them fear my wrath, when I got fired
from the shop.
You made me feel special when you did my hair.
You brought me Peach Snapple, whenever I
wanted.

You know who you are.
I thank you for making me a star.
I thank you for making me feel special.

I Am to

I Am the daughter of A and S.
I am the sister of those guys.
The cousin to them.
I AM the wife of him.
Mother to her.
Daughter to her.
Neice to them.
Daughter-in-law to them.
Friend to the circle.
Friend to her and him.
Teacher of them.
Inspirational and motivational to them.
I write for him.
I write for them.
I write for her.
I write for me.
And I write for him.
I laugh with her.
I laugh with all.
I trust no one.
but
I respect all.
I appreciate it all as much as I can.
I love with my heart in my hand.
&

I give a hug.
Sometimes I need a hug.
I give a hand.
Sometimes I need a hand.
I forgive
&
wish I was forgiven.
I love and wish
To be loved.
I don't share.
But I'll give you it all
and you won't know.
I pray for the best for
Me and for you.
What I made of,
Is a bit of salt, a bit of sugar and a bit of pepper.
That's what my mother told me.

Epis

A spice or spices,
That makes food taste nice,
I grew up on tasting in my mother's kitchen with
rice.
The epis could be savory or it could be spicy.
But it would always be tasty.
Full of my mother and my father's people.
People from the North and the South.
Spices that can heal and calm the soul.
Epis.
Smell the spice.
Smell the culture.
Smell the people.
Licking fingers.
Sauce drizzled over rice.
Chicken that tastes like heaven.
Seafood that's full of citrus and sun.
Holidays are built around a table full of epis and
love.
Seasoning hits your senses as you walk into her
house.
Black rice with shrimp, pumpkin soup with
pasta,
White rice with Sauce Pwa Nwa, Tasso with
pikliz,

Boulette or Macaroni Gratine, Bannann Peze
and Lambi.
Sweet oh sweet Kremas or Pain Patate.
Epis makes our souls sing.
Sing at the table,
We bring our souls, we bring our hearts,
We bring the ancestors through the food.
I bring my ancestors through my food.
My epis is made up of me and everyone behind
me.
Epi the epis in me.

Comme-ci Comme-ça

Life can be a little bit of
Comme-ci comme-ca.
Life at its best can make you feel like
It's a little bit of this or a little bit of that.
But life has always been the best of what you
make it.
Making it great, with exactly what you got.
You have to decide that your life is more than
just a little bit of this and a little bit of that.
Life is meant to be lived and it is meant to have
flashing lights.
It should bring you joy as much as possible.

You should be creating as much as possible,
trying to do the things that make you feel good.
Feel good in your soul, feel good in your heart.
I don't care if you are from here or from there,
Life should make you want to stare.
Stare at pictures that remind you of the best that
you gave and the best that you got, because you
gave the best that you had.
Come and see and come inside the world that
you have created.
Created to be the best that you can have.

Regular Life

I was born,
You were born,
We all were born to live.
Born to live a great life.
A life where we decide what positively great
experiences we want to feel.
A life where we decided what the dreams are.
Look around at all the success.
Those were choices,
Choices that said, "I'm not living a regular life".
A life where we are just going on with what was
given.
A life where we just take what is given.
A life where we are not thinking.
But we are born to live.
Live a long and prosperous life.
That does not mean, there won't be strife or
there won't be trials or errors.
But a prosperous life where we learn from the
errors and grow.
Where we plant seeds and have beautiful
harvests.
Or even make beautiful trees.

I am more than regular,

You are more than regular,
We are more than regular.
We are spectacular, look at us shine.
You shine,
I shine,
We all shine.

Sum

I've made choices.
Some good choices.
Some bad choices.
I made the decisions
that reflected what I was feeling.
My feelings always moved me through the
windows and some ceilings.
But many of those decisions cost me many
different life winnings and blessings.
I learned from the lost and worst resolutions.
I learned that life is meant for the living and not
for the frightened.
Only the eager, believer and doer wins.
Only the one who knows who they are in the
face of a storm gets to begin.
Begin a new way of life for themselves and their
kin.
I'm trying to make these next parts, about the
lessons that I learned from the sum of my
decisions.
I'm trying to live like a Queen with her King.
I'm trying to take everything.
And make everything a joy to live in.
I'm trying to bring laughter in the summer,
winter and spring.

I'm trying to experience all the bliss that God
can bring.
In the name of the Father and the Son and the
Holy Spirit, please forgive me of past sins.
So that the sum of my negatives can be forgiven.
And let the new choices be blessed and dressed
in the finest linen with the perfect sentiments.
Sentiments for me and my kindred.
My new choices, decisions, understanding and
actions are now rewritten because I believe that
I've been forgiven.
I've made atonement and have gone into
covenant.
A covenant that can not be broken.
A covenant with the one who blesses, creates
and generates all of my best and most precious
requests.
The requests that are and have been answered
right on time.
The time is now and I accept it.
I'm grateful for it.
cause I'm finally getting it all
and I'm even getting more than what I've prayed
for.
It's the sum.
The sum of my choices.
The sum of my praises above.
The sum of my belief.
The sum of my relief.

My choice was to rejoice, even when I didn't
have it all.
My choice was to be obedient to the law.
My choice was to remember the call.
My choice was to ask for forgiveness when I
knew I was wrong.
My choice is to believe and receive now.
My choice is to be sure now.
My choice is to know now.
I feel good now.
I'm ready now.
I know now.
It's all good now and
I am thankful and grateful, more than I've ever
been.
It's the sum